GW00375309

QUANTUM SHEEP

QUANTUM SHEEP

Valerie Laws

PETERLOO POETS

First published in 2006
by Peterloo Poets
The Old Chapel, Sand Lane, Calstock,
Cornwall PL18 9QX, U.K.

© 2006 by Valerie Laws

The moral rights of the author are asserted in accordance
with the Copyright, Designs and Patent Act, 1988

All rights reserved.   No part of this publication may be
reproduced, stored in a retrieval system, or transmitted,
in any form or by any means, electronic, mechanical,
photocopying, recording or otherwise without the prior
permission in writing of the publisher.

A catalogue record for this book is available
from the British Library

ISBN 1-904324-35-5

Printed by 4word Ltd,
Unit 15, Baker's Park, Cater Road, Bristol BS13 7TT

ACKNOWLEDGMENTS

Acknowledgements are due to Arts Council England North East, with thanks, for funding *Quantum Sheep*, a project actualised at Whitehouse Farm, Northumberland: to farmer Donald Slater for his time and help, and to his (less co-operative) sheep. The poem / project was featured on BBC Radio 4's *Today, News Quiz, National Poetry Day – a Peregrination, Pick of the Week, Pick of the Year*, as well as 18 other radio stations, 5 TV channels, 13 periodicals, and more than 30 websites worldwide.

To Guy's & St Thomas' Charity who funded the commission *Embedded in the Body* as "Window of Art". Four of the haiku are displayed on the windows of the Knowledge & Information Centre, St Thomas' Hospital, London, using computer-controlled electroluminescence by elumin8. Thanks to Liz Fairclough, KIC manager, and Karen Sarkissian, Guy's & St Thomas' Charity, for giving me this exciting opportunity and 6,000+ new readers per month.

Big Frocks was commissioned and animated by Cornwell Internet for Durham Literature Festival Website. *Olives* was commissioned by the Lit & Phil Library, Newcastle, for National Poetry Day. *TAG* was commissioned and broadcast by BBC World Service.

Acknowledgments are also due to the editors of anthologies *North by North East* (Iron, 06, ed. Cynthia Fuller & Andy Croft), *Sand 2* (ed Kevin Cadwallender), *Out of Order* (Zebra for New Word Order), *Miracle & Clockwork* (ed. James Roderick Burns): and journals, *Envoi, Pennine Platform, iota, Frogmore Papers, Other Poetry*.

Special thanks to Kate Griffin, who launched a thousand sheep and many other adventures. Thanks also to Poetry Vandals (especially Kate Fox; Hell's Belle, stand-up poet and mate) for giving me my rowdiest, raunchiest gigs.

Supported by
The National Lottery®
through Arts Council England

In loving memory of Sheila and Lindsay Laws

CONTENTS

After Häagen-Dazs

Chocolate, coffee, fruit; their day's gone by.
Our adult senses long for something new –
Give us ice cream that tastes of summer sky.

Or the scent of a lover's skin, soft as a sigh,
When fingers touch where rough winds never blew.
Chocolate, coffee, fruit; their day's gone by.

We want the wet kiss of rain when earth is dry
To water our parched mouths; or the blinding blue-
Flavoured ice cream that tastes of summer sky

Give us cornets smoky with Lapsang or Earl Grey,
Spring sundaes shy with violets! It's true,
That chocolate, coffee, fruit, have had their day.

Ice cream that tastes of grass will get us high,
Like the flavour of meadows in the stalks we chew
Lying in poppy fields under a summer sky.

New books, clean sheets, a waking city; I'd buy
Ice cream that tastes of these, or a summer sky.
Chocolate, coffee, fruit? Their day's gone by.

Into Thin Air

I bought myself an air ticket
To the air guitar championships
In Finland. There I met him,
And love was in the air.
Our fingers strummed
Rippling airs on infinitely
Fine strings, as we made
Beautiful silence together.
Powerful riffs moved the Earth
Undetectable on the Richter scale;
Our amps went to minus eleven.
Sweat ran from our writhing bodies
As we soundlessly played,
Giving it our all.
I was walking on air. I wanted
To mime my love from the rooftops,
Semaphore his perfection
To the world. But it was not to last.
He said he needed air, and that I
Was just an airhead; we rowed
Noiselessly, lipreading terrible
Accusations from each other. But
it didn't clear the air. He left me,
Appropriately, at the air terminal.
Now I listen incessantly to the tapes
rolling out the inaudible splendour
Of our duets. I'm almost sure
He's left me with a phantom pregnancy
But it can never fill my empty arms,
My empty heart. My fingers ache
From spelling out unheard laments
As my air guitar silently weeps.

Wonderbra!

After he dumped me,
I felt a little flat. My life
Needed perking up.
So, in search of something
Uplifting I turned to
Wonderbra!
I let Wonderbra handle everything,
Relaxed into its cupped hands,
Let it brace me up while
It carried my troubles for me.
It was fantastic. Suddenly
I was transformed, I had
Direction, Wonderbra pointed
The way. With its firm support,
I began to venture out. I followed
As Wonderbra led the way
Into every party. The trouble was,
I sometimes felt Wonderbra
Collected all the admiring glances,
The accidental arm-brushings,
While I stood behind. I felt
Unworthy to be with Wonderbra.
Then one night, a man
Sought me out, chatted, invited,
Seduced me back to his place.
Deftly, he removed my Wonderbra;
Left me drooping, and vanished
With it into the bedroom,
My false, deceiving Wonderbra:

I'm glad I've got it off my chest.

Not wine-dark

There, in the meat of the wave,
Where the water thickens
Bunching its muscle to leap,
That green,
That is the sea's true colour.

The silver the sun slicks on,
All dazzle and gleam,
The blues, violets and greys
The sky lends, these the sea wears:

In its cold and boundless heart,
The oceans flesh
Is the deep true green
Of crystallised
Angelica, whose flowers
White as wavecaps,
Storm the cliffs.

Divorcing the Guinea Pigs

My husband introduced me to divorce.
There was a lot of it about; I'd seen it
Being passed round at parties. Smugly,
I insisted I didn't need it. But
He made me try it. At first, pain, nausea,
Flashbacks. Then I got a taste for it:
Now its become a habit. I've become
The Zsa Zsa Gabor of Tyneside.

I divorced our house, despite its absolute
Fidelity over seventeen years together.
The guilty party this time, I took up with
A younger, slimmer, house which was
Conveniently detached. Our Habitat table,
Getting thin on top, its joints arthritic,
Eloped with a friend with my blessing.

Divorcing the Guinea Pigs was inevitable.
We never really communicated, but I cited
Unreasonable behaviour; squealing, hay
On the carpet. Next the piano. Mental cruelty.
Seven years of 'The Snowman' brought me
To meltdown; and I didn't like the nagging
Shrew it made me. But I do know where to stop:
Amicable separation from my teenage children,
With frequent visiting rights, no maintenance.

Out there

'Promise me I'll never have to go
out there again,' says Carrie Fisher
to her new-found, late-found fiancé
in *When Harry Met Sally*. Meaning
the whole dating thing. Well, I'm
out there, again. Out there
without a prompter, or a net,
or any other metaphorical support.

What I do have is my dating self.
Unfortunately, she's been in a coma
for twenty-five years. Painfully prodded
awake, like Austin Powers, she's stuck
in the seventies. Hankering for Marc Bolan,
pretty, non-threatening boys. Wishing
she was Bowie-bisexual, divinely decadent.
Flinching from her reflection, distorted
in the faces of middle-aged men.

Unable to cope with the loss of a quarter century
she longs to snog on sofas or in doorways,
her arms inside his coat, his patchouli blending
with her Aqua Manda, opening her eyes
to his Mascara'd eyes, perverse like *Cabaret*,
innocent like Bambi, reflecting the face
she still wears inside her head.

The Dulux Colour Chart as Pornography

Furtive in B&Q, I scan the shelves for
'The perfect partner. Like to do something
new?' Farrow and Ball tempts me, the name
pungent with farmyard coupling. But
it has to be Dulux, 'shaped to fit your hand,
first time, every time.' Here, in glossy
full colour spread, 'all you need
to achieve a perfect high —' and I'm
heating gently, my mind in steamy rooms,

pure indulgence, soft caress, double cream

I suck the names like melon balls,
the juices running, 'evoking lush aromas
of cherry and mango'. I'm stroking

'smooth and creamy, luxurious silk,'
buttersilk, buttermilk, summersatin.

I can feel them warming my bedroom,

soft, sugared, lilac love; desire

coming with me into the bathroom,

wild, honeygold, sunkissed yellow,
sensual, sexy, sassy pink.

In my fantasy I would have them all,
all over the house, on every wall,

tribal dance, white heat. After dark

on the bare floor, bold, rich, earthy,
rustic, roasted red, a celebration of
'the look I love, the toughness I need',
the lick of paint.

Big Frocks
(or A Tale of Two Cities)

(commissioned for Durham Litfest Website)

Top party city? Not Rio, not Newcastle, but Venice,
A centuries-long *ballo en maschera*. Look through
The lace mask of the Bridge of Sighs, at the boned
Bodices and crinolined cupolas of San Marco,
Santa Maria della Salute's hooped skirt. The city
Is a party! Down the Grand Canal's blue carpet,
Every palazzo is a big, Oscar-night frock, gilded
Pink and peach, taffeta and tulle, voile and velvet;
White braid balusters, windowbox corsages. Trailing
Muddied hems with superb aplomb, these shameless
Beauties carry their peeling stucco like finest
Devore. What is a dress, but a mask for the body?
What is a building, but a mask for the many? Mists
Of chiffon veil the canals, steel-sharp gondolas pin
Their satin ribbons. Bells swing their shining skirts,
Dancing music over the city like glitter dust.

Where Venice floats, Durham is rooted: bells rock
The cathedral tower, making stone quicken, long
To dance. From the north west, the tower is a bride,
Solemn and modest, her two bridesmaids allowed
A little frivolity. The castle is tight-laced above
The full skirt of its mound. Cinched by the river's
Simple silver belt, this northern beauty dreams
Of letting rip. It's time to celebrate, dare to don
Mask and motley, let the streets run with poetry and wine,
Until Venice is known as 'the Durham of the south'.

Quantum Sheep
a haik-ewe

(Spray painted on the backs of live sheep, who rewrote the poem as they moved about; project funded by Arts Council North East, December 02 June 03. Over 8 billion combinations possible.)

CLOUDS GRAZE THE SKY;
BELOW, SHEEP DRIFT GENTLE
OVER FIELDS, SOFT MIRRORS,
WARM WHITE SNOW.

Four of the Poems Generated:

CLOUDS OVER MIRRORS:
WHITE FIELDS SOFT BELOW.
SNOW SHEEP DRIFT THE SKY,
WARM, GRAZE GENTLE.

SNOW CLOUDS THE SKY OVER
GENTLE FIELDS; SHEEP GRAZE;
SOFT WHITE MIRRORS BELOW
DRIFT WARM.

WARM DRIFT, GRAZE GENTLE,
WHITE BELOW THE SKY;
SOFT SHEEP MIRRORS FIELDS,
SNOW CLOUDS OVER.

SHEEP BELOW; OVER, DRIFT
SOFT SNOW CLOUDS;
WARM MIRRORS GRAZE
WHITE FIELDS, THE SKY GENTLE.

Embedded in the Body

(A suite of five embedded haiku)

1. BONE

We carve our own faces; our muscles knead
the **bone** that **lives in us,** with rage or joy.
As waves erode **warm sea coral,** planing
down **its growing wall** so emotion's tide
shapes our defences, moulds the skull
which holds our wish to smile.

2. BRAIN

The knowledge **London cabbies have**
gives them **brains as big as the city –**
the hippocampus coils its seahorse
tail in tendrils of memory,
A maze within a maze.

3. EMBRYO

Embryos live **our evolution:**
from cell to gill-slit **minnow,**
tadpole, yolk-fed chick, to furred,
tailed **monkey; boy or girl,** we told
our first story in secret, before
our tongue grew words.

4. TRANSPLANT

The body stays true to the lost heart.

remembers that perfect fit of valve,

chamber, cell. Sedated, it cradles

the changeling heart, always doubts

the **beautiful flushed fist knocking**

on the body's walls, sharing its blood

5. EYES

Humans see eye to eye with the octopus,

a **brainy** mollusc matching our cornea,

retina, lens. It **makes a submarine** garden

we use to hunt, to kill it. **Spineless?**

Yet it meets our eyes as death bites.

The Sound of No Music

In life there is no music
To warn us of danger,
Or sudden love. No strings
Start sobbing, no shark-attack
Knife beats, no gothic
Heart-clutching crescendo
Tell us, don't go down those stairs!
The shocks
Of burglar in your bedroom, metal
Railing through your chest, bus
Driving through your car, all
Happen, like sudden joy,
To totally inappropriate soundtracks
Or none at all. Blackbirds practise
Their phrasing, soap operas bleat,
A toilet flushes, as our life changes
Or ends, as we think, more
Than our pre-cinema ancestors did,
How, how can this happen, and to me?

Seeing Myself Think

Last night I saw myself think;
I caught myself out. Just
As I went to sleep
I saw the ideas, a sea
Of winking sparks like mackerel
Under the moon or the flutter
Of cameras flashing
In a dark auditorium; or
The bioluminescence
Of deep sea creatures signalling
In the black cold. Each thought
Was a light leaping a synapse
Where pairs of nerve cells
Reached out to each other, their touch
Kindling. Whole galaxies
Of consciousness glittered before
My eyes.

And I saw myself thinking, our sun
Might be a spark of thought
In an enormous mind
Which sees its thoughts flash
In the birth and death of stars.

More than Half

After he left, I slept in half the bed,
In a house that had doubled in size.
Now my new house, my own
House, my white drapes billowing
With light like muslin with rich curd,
Sun melting the wood on my rocking chair,
Seems more than half the house we shared.
I find I'm using more than half the bed,
Spreading like warm butter over
Crusty white cotton, two-timing the pillows
At random: I wake aslant, a leg
At each corner. I'm expanding like new bread
To fill my own space; I'm more than half
Of what we were, twice what I was.

No Fear of Flying

Now that he is no longer here
To protect me, I am no longer afraid
To fly. Turbulence, sudden veers,
Judderings, leave me serene,
Enjoying cappuccino clouds.
Now I walk on the beach alone,
I no longer fear dogs,
Who no longer attack me
As they did us. I exchange
Cheerful greetings with owners,
Whose grinning dogs kick up
Spray while the sea
Rolls over lazily for me to
Stroke its belly. Without him
Beside me in the car,
No road rage, no raised fingers
Or voices, but eye contact
And 'please go ahead' gestures. Now
I have to catch spiders myself,
There seem to be fewer of them.
Now the only thing I need a man
To protect myself against
Is men.

Olives

Olives are fruit for women –
They belong to those who like
Taking trouble. Wry, difficult,
Salty, with oil-bruised flesh
To lubricate the mouth, a stone
With a point to prick the tongue,
They are bitter but generous.

Olives are fruit from the goddess –
The gift of Athene, dark drupes
Bled from knotted veins
Of ancient, silver trees, yet
Bleeding virgin oil, golden as wine,
Given freely at first pressing. Ripe,
Like the haemorrhoids of pregnancy,
They cling to their steed, reluctant
To launch each crafted keel. From
Lands of machismo, vendetta, corrida,
Olives endure, bring light, healing,
Nourishment, peace, keep the lamp
Burning, the sacred feminine alive.

Passenger Announcement

'This train has a no smoking policy. In addition,
Coach C has been allocated as a quiet coach, in which
Mobile phones and personal stereos are not allowed.
Passengers who suck their fingers, one by one,
With noisy and overtly sexual relish
After eating crisps
Are asked to use Coach E; while those travelling
With bright, overstimulated children talking
Particle physics in piercing high pitched voices,
Are advised Coach H is designated for their use.
Coach I is for passengers who ingest
Their own bodies, viz. cuticles, fingernails, nose linings,
Spleens etc. May I remind such passengers the buffet
Is open for the sale of hot snacks and beverages,
Marginally more nutritious and vastly more profitable.
Obese passengers intending to wobble or sweat
Are asked to use Coaches J and K, and further,
To refrain from blocking the aisles. All window seats
Are reserved for passengers who will be noticing
The late sun igniting the hawthorn berries, silvering
The rose bay willow herb seed fluff, and turning to amber
The occasional basking fox. Thank you.'

Border Wars, Belsay Castle

Three children with names from Harrods
And three toy guns
Stalk each other. shooting through empty
Windows. Their parents stroll smiling
Among the ruins as if among prize crops
They've raised. Struggling
To climb, the smallest girl pulls herself
Up, stands on a truncated pillar.
'Playing statues?' says her mother.
They are face to face, equal heights,
The girl's cheek smooth and plump
As a rosehip. Smiling, she raises
Her gun and fires
Into her mother's face.
The late sun warms the castle walls,
Bloodying the hawthorns.

Mating Sharks

'Mating is violent. Pursued by the males,
the females panic and become
trapped in shallow water.'

We females lead the males
Into the shallows, where the water's
Skin, our sky, is blinding silver,
Where the sea is hot as the need
That drives us. Our thrashing tails
Stir up sand which glitters like scales,
Tickling our bellies; our fins break
Surface to the stroking of dry air.

'The male seizes a female, sinking his teeth
into her fin. They struggle until the male
coils his body around hers and inserts
sperm into her cloaca.'

I lead my chosen male by the nose
As we twine like kelp in a gale,
Our bodies strong and yielding,
Our toothed skins rubbing together,
Created our own electric storm. He holds on,
Those beautiful jaws drawing no blood
Whose scent might distract us
From this rarer frenzy. I wrap him round me
Like a knot of shining muscle, suck
The life out of him, to spark
Like flakes of mica in my belly, like the flash
Of mackerel. Hunger floods back, and I ache
For the taste of flesh.

Hang up your connection

Would you like to hang up your connection?

Yes   No

A spark of late sun ignites my wedding ring
As it turns, rising and falling, the contact
Broken as the sea swallows it like a pill.

Would you like to hang up?

                                    No,
Don't hang up. Let those words unspool
Onto the tape, the wheel turning, winding
Hanks of secrets behind its tiny window.

Yes   No

The circuit of years breaks, our private language
No longer current, my thoughts turning
Between love and hate, pity and fear.

Do you wish to delete checked mails?

                                    No.
I keep reading your letters, hoarding
Every contradiction, obsessive as a lover,
As the printer rolls its wheels of evidence.

Truth   Lies

What you said, didn't say. What I
Heard you say. Weeks, months, circle
Like hungry wolves too weak to pounce.
Your car circles my house, I circle the streets
Watching for your car.

Do you wish to hang up your connection?
The cursor spirals, homing in on

Yes

Freezes a moment, then moves on, freed.

Skydiving Frogman

I am the man who swam through fire and air
With only an aqualung to help him fly.
I did not stand a chance.   It was not fair.

My fins and wetsuit made the rangers stare,
When far inland they saw my body lie
After the clash of water, fire and air.

It seemed impossible I should be there,
A neoprene Lucifer fallen from the sky
To watery, fiery death. It was not fair

The fire-fighting 'copter hovered where
I swam beneath the waves, sucked me up high
Like a woodlouse in a hoover. Fire scorched the air

'Til water, and I, quenched it. I swear,
I'd never choose a surreal way to die
That people laughed at. Tell me, is that fair?

Killed by four elements, earth, water, fire and air
Now mocked in my martyrdom. I'm the guy
Treated like a freak at a country fair,
The Darwin award my prize. Does no-one care?

Capri; Last Summer

Blue-green as chopped thick glass,
the sea which flung those sudden
haughty cliffs, flaunting
impossibly white villas.

Holding on as the boat bucked,
looking for the tiny bloody fingers
of true coral burning
where wave met stone, our hands
on the warm wet wood. His
so unlike mine, fingernails
flat and broad, thick wrist,
as if he belonged
to a different species. My hair
blew around the camera
as I tried to hold it all
in that small box

Gulls jigged like blown snow,
dark against bright sky.

House Doctoring

Houses are the opposite of prostitutes;
To sell, they must be covered
In a burka of beige. There are house doctors
Who will tell you how to neutralise your house,
Expunge your life from it, your special joys,
Those tearing tears on the stairs.
I have tried; but my house keeps breaking out.

'This is the sitting room, barley white, note the new Upvc
windows;' viewers troop around, eyeing and prodding,

Can they hear my skull collection,
the rattling of mandibles in the cupboard?

'This is a large single, or a small double room,' I say
loudly to drown the squabbling of my stuffed birds
confined reluctantly to the wardrobe. A bathroom door
flushes 'sexy pink' as I hastily swing it shut;

the yellow hall plays 'who likes butter?'
beneath its mantle of magnolia.

'What a big bedroom!' they say, as the bright sarong
smelling of sea and suncream bursts from a drawer.
They will need bat's ears to pick up the faint squeaks
of past orgasms, infant wails, jostling like Roman ghosts
hungry for forgetfulness.

I have castrated my house, but it still yowls
Like a randy tom, pulsing with unwanted life,
Spraying the scent of years over all my efforts,
Putting off the putters with its gamey, florid,
Fleshy, fat, ageing colours, curves and angles,
Refusing to be put down.

Tag

(Commissioned in 2003 by BBC and broadcast on Outlook, World Service debate on graffiti art.)

WE CARRY OUR VOICES IN CANS,

SHOUT OUR NAMES IN COLOUR;

OUR LIVING EPITAPHS BURN

ON COLD DEAD WALLS. EACH

SCARLET SCREAM, BLACK BELLOW,

YELLOW YELL, BLAZES THE UNHEARD

MESSAGE: I *WAS* HERE!

Blue Sky Express

Suddenly spilled into light abroad at last,
we've travelled between worlds. We fell
asleep in gloomy Paris suburbs chopped
into high-rise chunks; our train has ruled
a line down France, unzipped
the country and fling open Cote D'Azur;
the azure coast, not sounding too high-flown
in French, where the telephone book is poetry
and political speeches expertly seduce.
And now there's this – hot sun, hot flowers,
hot colours, scent of rosemary, cigales
purring! Abroad at last, we're suddenly
spilled into light, a sky too blue to express.

Swimming with Jellyfish

The sea curdles into a spawn of moony jellies,
Blown inshore by a Baltic wind. Suspended
Like a flush of used condoms, the water is thick
With them, slowly pulsing, breathing water
Into empty bellies, their clear curves
Like cataract-veiled lenses, fringed
With tiny lashes. Inside, four violet crescents,
Symmetrical in pairs like chromosomes,
Glow neon. They have repulsed the swimmers,
But I go in, push through them with my hands,
Feel them cool and smooth against my skin.
I am aspic'ed in living tapioca pudding,
Feeling only pleasure, a myriad stings unfelt
And unintended. The sea slows, reduced
To jellied consommé, stirred from within.

Antinous at the River

I am about to become a god,
Baptise myself into my religion
By total immersion. I hope it will be quick
And relatively painless. Cleansing, anyhow.
I choose this death that will deify me,
But I do not want it, this metamorphosis
That will be thrust upon my sodden corpse
As so much unwanted honour has been
Plastered on me like river mud.

Standing on the bank, sun warming my back,
I can see the river's rich green broth
Twitching with life like a horse's skin
When flies bite. It will be hard to drown in,
Like gulping green olive oil, gagging,
My youth and strength fighting for a life
My soul is weary of. But I pray
To myself, the god I know Hadrian
Will proclaim me, that the river slime
Will wash away the snail-tracks of his tongue
And the sweat of his imperial hands, dissolve
And soak away the beauty which made him
Love me. It is easier to die than to say no
To an Emperor.

Over there a girl washes her legs; children play,
Splashing. I could have married, sired sons,
Been ordinary, lost my looks through work
And hearty eating. Hadrian worships me:
Soon, all the Empire will be forced
To do likewise. Let them. I will not feel
Their sticky, pleading hands
On the cold statue that replaces me. Helpless,
I choose divine power, earthly death, eternal life.

Aphrodite rises from the Foam

Aphrodite rises from foam like salty cappuccino
grossed out and spitting. She feels like crying
over the spilled milk from her father's scrotum,
scythed off and flung to sea to give her life.
The sea enjoyed the taste of him so much,
it burped this radiant goddess from its belly;
but what does she do now?
The ocean's not the kind of mother you call up
for advice, though to be fair, she'll never
turn up at sports day in an embarrassing hat.
But for now, that's academic. Her daughter's
out there, alone, combing divine semen
from her rippling hair, knowing only
she's something to do with something called 'love.'
Her new-washed eyes turn landwards:
it's clean and dry, anything but salty, and she's off
on a jetski, strimming the foam, scything
her mother's waves, and she could wish the land
would never reach her now. Wind buffs her skin
with wafts of warm thyme, she's high on speed,
thinking, so this is what love is!

Book Abuse

My parents' generation cared for books.
They were a luxury, to be dusted
Or kept behind glass, like old folk
Arranged in a nursing home, preserved
Like pickles.

I have the luxury of ill-treating my books.
I manhandle them like
Hardy toddlers, romp with them, throw
Them about, curl up with them, share
Drinks and apples with them,
Give them rough love.

Chainsaw Massacre

(after Shakespeare's Sonnet 73)

This time of year when I would hope to see
Green buds on boughs that shake against the cold,
I hear the growling chainsaw gnaw each tree
To a stump, brought low for growing too high, too old,
Or daring to touch the net of wires which hang
Connecting each house to a stark dead pole.
'Bare ruined choirs where late the sweet birds sang'?
Bare, ruined indeed, this street without a soul.
No room for trees, now rows of sleek cars stand
Glittering where once there spread full leafy shade.
Sycamore, chestnut, beech, are on too grand
A scale; polluted air for clean's a dirty trade.
But perching on wires, the birds still sing as sweet,
While our silent voices thread between their feet.

Poet's Apprentice

(for Ian McMillan)

I got the funding; appointed him my mentor.
At first it was a doddle, going to readings,
Topping up his glass, handing him phrases
On cue, picking up the odd dropped image.
He let me try my hand at haiku, told me
In a year or two, I could move on to sonnets,
Maybe.

Then one day it all went pear-shaped.
He went out, leaving me to polish
His rough drafts, check the spelling.
I thought, maybe I could spell
As well as him. That was it. The pen
Came to life in my hand, words flowed from it
And pages flew up like doves, unstoppable.
I was thigh-deep in poetry when he came back,
Saw paper oozing under the door, burst in
To be knocked down by an avalanche
Of epic ballads. He stilled the flow
With words of calm command, made me
Clean up the mess with a bucket of tippex.

    I'm back on haiku
    And topping up his glass with
    Red wine from a box.

The Flatpack Baby Blues

Well I got me a flatpack baby
Like the one they got next door –
Got so many special features
I don't know what half of them are for.

Got a all-over wipe-clean surface,
Got a worktop that's state of the art.
Brain like Einstein's, and a cute face –
A smile that goes right to my heart.

Got a full set of instructions,
Got me a lifetime guarantee;
Says here, 'to effect construction'
I won't need no PhD.
          Thank God.

Chose 'black ash' with blue eye fittings,
Hair red as mine's been dyed;
Soon there was my son sitting,
Good as gold – ain't never cried.
          No man, not once.

But something's wrong, some odd bits
Got left lying on the floor
Like always with assembly kits –
Wonder what those bits were for?

Now my baby's looking at me
With those big cold baby blues.
I keep trying to ring the factory
But it ain't no goddamn use;

Just recorded voices, man.
Ain't no one there that's real;
I'm left to do the best I can.
No-one cares how I feel.

Packing and Unpacking

What do I really need?
I must select from all this life-hoard,
edit my sprawling possessions
down to a neat bundle, enough
for a week, my unknown life
in that place. Lists. Heaps. Layers
of clothes, shoes, cosmetics;
the open bag, lazily yawning
on the bed, waits to be filled.

What have I brought?
Arrived, I excavate the small
collection I have carried here,
place each object in a room
which waits for me to colour it in.
The bedside table, bathroom shelf,
wardrobe, coat hooks, all clothed
by and in me. On the bed,
the unpacked bag yawns, exhausted,
empty, waiting to be filled.

Silver Sonnet

Our silver wedding shone on the horizon;
But how to celebrate this special day?
We wanted to do something more surprising
Than champagne dinner, family party: say,
A visit to Capri, oh, how romantic,
Soft air, sea curdling sweet and blue below:
The Vendée, pounded by the wild Atlantic,
Whale-watching at the south pole in the snow:
Venice, of course, that beauty most serene:
The world our oyster, we the precious pearl,
A quarter century to buff up its sheen . . .
And then I caught him with another girl.
Surprisingly, it was fun to celebrate
My silver wedding with my best girl mate.

Not Waving

The foreign sea is not waving,
Nor drowning anyone.
It does not rampage
Up and down the beach,
Eating our shoes and towels.
It holds me like a mother,
Safe and warm, shows me
Funny bright fish
To tickle me, lets me see
All of itself, shot taffeta
Colours like the party dress
My mother made me,
Blue violet green.

My north sea is the colour of bruises,
Its rough like boys
You're not allowed to play with.
Cold, opaque, and rowdy,
Shouting all night, heaving
Lumps of concrete about.
It swipes anglers off piers, paddlers
Off beaches, trawlers
From the surface. Its mad, bad,
Dangerous and unknowable.

But it's the one I go home to.

Queue Jumping

Phoning from France, my son
Reminds me how some people
Jump the queue,
Push in front of you,
And grab your death.

'Remember that bungee jump I did?
From the rickety crane?
At the little French fair?
Someone died on it next day.'

It was waiting to happen, and I am
Glad it was to someone else's son.
In my case, it was a pater noster,
A vertical loop of stacked lifts,
Open cells we students hopped
In and out of. One day I missed
My cue, stayed on, and went up
And over the top.
Sudden total black, deafening
Grinding of unseen machines,
The suddenly flimsy walls
Shaking; terror, then relief
As light leapt in with me.
I never did it again. Nor
Did the girl who tried it
Soon after, when the walls
Collapsed.

'They could hear the screams
For miles. They were picking
Bone splinters out of the gears
For weeks.'

The pity, the relief, I dodged
That one. The wondering, what
Will I get, when it's my turn next
And no-one pushes in.

Mothering

We clutch each other, laughing, on the beach.
Her shoes are drenched, her skirt and legs all splashed;
She jumped a tiny stream, but failed to reach
The other side, she's wet but unabashed
'Where did you leave the car?' she asks.
Her hands are worn and seamed with tiny cracks
By years of skilful, cheerful household tasks.
Her mind wiped clean, her skin now bears the tracks.
'Lovely to see you, you know, I'm proud of you.'
She says. 'Where did you leave the car?'
I try to think of something we can do;
She strides for miles, I can't walk very far.
She can't hold a thought, a plot, or information,
But keeps insisting she must go to the station
To get home to her mam and dad, long dead,
But now alive again inside her head
With me, my father — but he's become two men,
Both with the same name; she asks again,
'The car, darling, whereabouts did you leave it?'
Her son's visit with his children brings her joy:
'I like that tall man!' Once her little boy.
Will I forget my children? I won't believe it!
We leave out parents lightly for a lover,
Then children fill our minds and hearts. No other
Tie as strong, surely? Yet we recover,
All else erased, the memory of our mother,
The first and last, morning and evening star,
Like mine, who asks again, 'Where did you leave the car?'

Liberace to his Lover's Plastic Surgeon

(after Shakespeare's Sonnet 3)

Look at him now, and tell the face you see
Now is the time that face should form another.
Let him look in the mirror and see me,
Let him be both my mirror and my lover.
Make his smile gleam just like mine, but younger,
Reflect me in his face, not just his eyes.
Give him a nose and chin like mine, but stronger,
To make him truly mine, despite the lies
I tell the press. I'll never have a son,
But my dollar-count is higher than the stars.
I'll pay, and pay again, to have just one
Heir to my face, which time already scars.

Nothing in my life is what it seems,
So carve for me the true man of my dreams.

Killed in Action

(from Government Accident Statistics)

While charging headlong up,
head back, eyes raised,
rushing to heaven
in a lover's bed;
or winging to a child, lifted by air
sharp and thick with screams,
or homing to the cool bath of linen
on hot skin, the snug music
of how that dress clings
like a song to a tune:

or while advancing, going
over the top and down, hit
in the heart by the crack
of the letterbox, or bayoneted
by that special key sliding
into the lock; with feet invisible
under a pregnant mound,
or lethally graceful puddles
of fabric, flaring skirts:

launched into sudden flight
ending too soon to grasp
that flight was theirs;
a thousand deaths a year
from climbing stairs.

MyDoom

He invaded my inbox:
I felt violated.
I gave him my edress,
He contaminated
My laptop with porn.
I felt like I'd dated
A rapist. But the guy was
Sorry he'd done it:
I gave him a virus.

Mine

(For three voices from three graves in a small Northumbrian churchyard;
Sarah, and her two husbands, both miners.)

Listen! Rooks, smuts on the sky's wet sheet; rain stotting down,
hissing like the copper boiling over
while I lie between two men, both mine.
– *She is mine, mine,*
~ *Sarah is mine!*
Buried before he died, my strong collier lad,
– *The earth breathed out and its ribs crushed mine,*
me hanging out his shirt, in a breeze stiff as a starched collar,
already a widow. Always washing,
boiling, soaping, possing, wringing, starching, pegging, ironing . . .
washing the blood and the coal dust of him,
white as dolly blued cotton. Claiming him back
from the mine, only to bury him again –
– *Our unborn bairns buried with me, like seeds to deep to grow.*
You'd always wanted Sarah, wanted me dead –
~ *I bided my time, mended her roof,*
and I mended his best shirt; one day I laughed, it stung like fat spat
from a burst sausage but –
~ *She'd mended.*
Mending, sewing, darning, hemming, knitting, smocking . . .
~ *She's take you flowers, then we'd go home to*
Yorkshire pudding: whisking, basting, roasting, baking,
– *claggy in the middle, crusty round about, rising like a rook to its nest!*
~ *The smell of the roast as we came back from church, and apple tart!*
   Sweet steam rising, the taste
– *of being alive! Earth in my mouth for so long!*
His spine like a stack of bobbins, he'd cough black phlegm
from long years down the pit. The mine took both their lives
and between them, they took mine.
~ *I watched her die; walked home, past the graves*
with their green glass chippings
Like the salts the bairns gave me at Christmas,

~ headstones wonky like the dead climbing out; from the mine,
– where the living worked under the dead,
winning the coal, losing their lives.
Now I lie between them, the young husband and the old.
– Which of us will she spend eternity with?
Listen! The earths hollow bones, creaking and aching.
– The one who kissed her first!
~ The one who held her dying!
I hear bairns running over the chippings. If they fall,
it'll not be me to wash their knees.
~ She's still my wife,
– my Sarah.
I'll not need to wash the sun's sticky fingerprints off.
– Choose me, Sarah, your lost young lover!
~ Choose me, Sarah, my lost old woman!
I gave you my tears, my bairns, my hands, my heart.
I loved you both, but you don't know
my neat, private bones, slender as new moons, strong as stone,
under the trees and the slowly breathing earth. No-one
calling me, no-one wanting me. This is my choice
Now, my time is mine.

'I've got a heifer to inseminate' (Ruth Archer)

(for Val McDermid)

You may be gay, you may be straight,
Your period may be five days late,
But all this trivia will have to wait
When you've a heifer to inseminate.

We all know there's nothing finer
Than to have your arm up a cow's vagina,
Though sod's law says, when you're up to your pits,
The phone will ring or the cow get the shits.

Your life may be a load of bull,
So use it! Prime that syringe full,
But before you plunge it deep within her,
Remember – flowers, chocolates, dinner.

Don't forget the etiquette that's necessary
When your hand becomes a bovine pessary;
Don't leave her complaining it's just not right,
That you never call, and you never write.

You need not flinch from an amorous encounter
With a cow expecting a bull to mount her –
What's never had is never missed,
She may prefer your latexed fist.

No heifer will ever say 'Oh, no' to our Ruth,
Her accent is false but she speaks the truth
When she says the way to enjoy a hot date
Is to find a heifer to inseminate.

Single Minded

My husband left: my friends all rallied round
With wine and love. They made the air resound
With lurid tales of marital disasters,
And cries of 'Never mind, all men are bastards!
You don't need him you're better off alone!'
And they were right. My ever faithful phone
Began to ring with publication offers,
Commissions, party invitations; coffers
Far from empty, a new house, trips abroad –
I sometimes longed for time just to be bored.
They all said how I'd blossomed, shown the swine
I didn't miss him: life was truly mine.

But then they started trying to pair me off!
My honest protests only made them scoff
Wherever I've been, it's, 'Any nice men there?'
Or, 'Why not have a lesbian affair?'
Why can't they see I'm happy to flirt and mingle,
But do really prefer a life that's single.
'There's someone out there waiting for you, dear';
That's not something of which, my friends, I'm dreaming.
It sounds more like a horror film, I fear;
The thought of someone out there, I run screaming.

S & M

Met a cute guy all dressed in leather,
Thought we could have some fun together,
But what I thought was a statement of fashion
Turned out to be the focus of his passion.
Now I'm all for having lashings of fun
But that S & M's not for everyone.
Don't get me wrong, I can take it,
But I got real pain, don't need to fake it.
Seems some folk just love to suffer,
Boy meets girl, and wants to handcuff her.
I said to him, this'd be flogging a dead horse,
He said, 'Yes, please, my place or yours?'
I said, I may be strange, but I like pleasure.
He said, between that and pain is hard to measure,
It's a real fine line, a real close call.
I said for me, that line's like the Berlin wall.
Set even one foot on no man's land,
I'll knock you down right where you stand.
You've as much hope of touching me with a flogger
As I have of becoming a marathon jogger.
I was still thinking there might be some common ground,
Where we could play around,
Get on down, but then I found he had a piercing,
Down there!
I couldn't believe what I was hearing, ladies,
You know how often you lose an earring!
If I say I want a stud in me,
I don't mean it literally!
It may be his lucky charm,
But I don't want to set off the metal alarm
When I fly, I'd just die of shame.
If that's what the real Prince Albert used,
No wonder the Queen was not amused.
No, man, I'll show you the meaning of pain,

If you come near me with that tomfoolery,
I don't go in for genital jewellery.
If you really want something to turn you shivery,
You should try having a forceps delivery;
It'd make even a masochist nervous,
When the doc comes at you with steel salad servers.
Pain's not for me; with that, I made tracks;
After all, I was late for my bikini line wax.

Orgasms are Easy

Since my baby left me,
I've learned to put up a shelf;
In fact, all the things he did for me,
I can do them for myself,
Because
Orgasms are easy, yes
Orgasms are easy, oh yes, yes,
But there's still one thing I miss.

If your baby leaves you,
You can learn to handle a drill,
You can find out how to drive a screw
And give yourself a thrill,
Because
Orgasms are easy, oh yes, yes,
I know how to please me, but
I just can't give myself a kiss.

For when the earth's stopped shaking,
And you've put your tool away,
There's a pair of lips still aching
For the game only two can play,
Because
Orgasms are easy, oh god yes,
I won't ever tease me,
I can't even hug and squeeze me, but
I just can't give myself a snog.

You can get all kinds of electrics
To put a swivel in your hips,
You can buy all sorts of bags of tricks,
But not electric lips,
Because
Orgasms are easy, oh, yes, yes,
Orgasms are easy, oh, no, no –
You need another mouth to do the job;
Yes, even a princess needs a frog.

Straight Talking

Men have a thing like a truncheon,
Women, more like a rose,
But when it comes to something to munch on,
Well, I've already got one of those.

Oh, women are sweet, and women are floral,
Men's hygiene sometimes runs amuck,
But when it comes to pleasures oral,
Why do I need a man to s-nog?

A woman can touch like a butterfly's wing.
A man, like being hit by a truck.
But when it gets down to that physical thing,
Why do I need a man for a f-ling?

Oh, women are good, and women are better,
Gay women have all the luck.
All men have is somewhere to put a French letter,
Why do we need a man to f-ix a date with?

Slim Volume

Sugar is made from sunlight,
Aspartame's made by boffins:
Who knows if drinking something 'lite'
Will hurry us to our coffins?
But if chemicals do breed cancer,
Still the decision to eat them's not hard;
We won't lose our sense of tumour
But we'll lose a lot of lard,

Because anything's better than being fat,
Yes, anything's better than that.

As your weight begins to drop
And the scales are no longer groaning,
And you try on clothes in a fashion shop,
You can hear weightier women moaning.
As that dress slides over you like a lovers tongue,
And you're slim, attractive, and shapely and young,
You might keep losing weight, for it's not just fiction
That even starvation can become an addiction,

But hey! Anything's better than being fat,
Yes, anything's better than that.

When you've a billiard ball bum,
They all say you look great;
But your boobs have become
Like raw eggs on a plate.
So you have silicon implants,
Your figure looks grand –
Then they migrate round your body
Till your head's full of sand,

But at least it's better than being fat,
Yes, anything's better than that.

So here's to losing the lumps
Down with grams, pounds and stones,
Let all visible bumps
Be your newly-found bones.
It's worth all the suffering,
The pain of denial,
To go into a shop, pick
The latest new style,
Go try it on, win the ultimate prize;
The words, 'This is too big,
I'll need a smaller size.'

Because anything's better than being fat,
Yes, anything's better than that.

The Wrong Sex

Since we met the other day,
My head's been a whirl –
You see, I really like you but
I wish you were a girl.

It's not that I'm a celibate
Or sapphically inclined;
It's just that I can't do anything
But like you for your mind.

If only you were a woman,
The things I could say
Like, 'Do you like me in this dress?'
Or 'Shall we go out, Saturday?'

I wish you were a woman,
As you sit there facing me;
I could smile into your eyes,
Confide in you over tea.

For we have so much in common,
So much we could share,
If we were just two women,
And sex didn't hang in the air.

You're nice, you're sweet, you're clever,
Full of exciting ideas –
But I know I could never kiss that mouth,
Or nibble on those ears.

Although your sparkling wit
Has me laughing like a drain,
I'd rather snog a total twit
Like Mel Gibson with no brain.

Men hear differently from women,
Whatever may be said;
A simple offer of friendship
Can sound like an invite to bed.

It's hard to sustain a friendship
After repelling their advance,
Hurting their tender pride
By telling them there's no chance,

No spark, no thrill,
No heat, no chill,
No glance, no slow dance,
No touch of the hand,
No grind of the hip,
No one night stand,
No pressure of lip,
No removal of dress,
No intimate caress,

No. This isn't going to work
Unless you become female,
Or emigrate, so we can talk
Exclusively by e-mail.

The Other Man

My rival is handsome, he's smooth as whipped cream,
He doesn't have stretchmarks like ripple ice cream,
He doesn't have bingo wings, saddlebags, tights,
He doesn't need tampax or always ultra nights.
I try to compete, but I don't think I can,
For the man I'm in love with's in love with a man.

I'm rubbish on football – why do cups have legs?
Why's that man offside, when he's still on the team?
Men drink beer without guilt, and eat two fried eggs,
And talk about engines powered by steam.
How can I compete? I don't see how I can,
When the man I'm in love with's in love with a man.

The crack in our romance has become a fissure,
My lover only thinks of HIM, starry eyed.
What can I do? Even going on Trisha
Won't get my man back batting on the right side.
I'm doomed to a life lived alone on the shelf,
For the man my lover's in love with's – himself.

Lips that touch liver

He's drop dead gorgeous, his eyes are divine,
But lips that touch liver never shall touch mine.
We're chewing the fat, but oh Lord deliver us
From the gristly chomping of a man who's carnivorous.

He's drop-dead gorgeous, his hair is divine,
But lips that touch liver never shall touch mine.
Is it too much to hope that gifts physical and mental
Could belong to a man with a yen for the lentil?

He's drop-dead gorgeous, he wears Calvin Klein,
But lips that touch liver never shall touch mine,
Though scoffing dead animals is technically lawful
To see him eat kidneys is literally offal.

He's drop dead gorgeous, his eyes are divine,
But lips that touch liver never shall touch mine.
If he wants my good lovin', he'll sign the pledge;
A man needs only one kind of meat and two veg.

In praise of small penises

It's not hard
To stand
Up for men who have nothing to guard
But the family jewel – well, sequin;
Let's give a warm hand
To those who have only a threeskin;
Whose cock is more of a chick,
More of a di- than a dick.

A man who can give you an inch
(Or two) can take you a mile high:
If you want an orgasmic explosion,
The G-spot's two inches inside –
Any more is just
Cervical erosion.

A penis mightier than the sword
Might make it in the world of porn;
The pawn like you find on a chessboard
We celebrate, pink and curled as a prawn.

(Hey, is that a hazelnut in your pocket,
Or are you just pleased to see me?)

Come on, show us what you haven't got,
Let's see the last budgie in the shop,
Whether erect or cutely dangled,
If you're not so much 'well hung'
As 'slightly strangled.'

Not so much a lunchpack
As a cocktail sausage –
A weeny wiener, a twinkle of a winkle,
A petite and two veg.

I don't want no Jake the Peg,
I don't want no extra leg;
I'd rather a man who'll lift a finger
That knows just when and where to linger.

Let's face it, he's easier to handle
As long as his technique is slick
If he dips the wick
Of a birthday cake candle.

A man who only wears A-fronts
Might not manage the stunts
Of a hen-night stripper:
So what if he isn't so wide,
He can give you a white-knuckle ride
On his little dipper.

'Hello, big boy, what a enormous gun,'
Might be O.K. as flattery.
Truth to tell, you'd get more fun
From something with a battery.

And after all,
Men whose endowments are small
Can take comfort when they recall
That lesbians perform miracles with no penis at all.

So cheer up men the gods forgot to endow,
Some of us can't live without you;
And of course men who are reading this now,
Of course, this poem isn't about you.

Sedna

(New planet discovered March 2004)

Eight planets, with sun and moon, smiled on our birth;
But far off in the dark, like a fist tightly curled,
Slept the goddess of oceans. Now for us on Earth,
She's come out fighting, she's rocking our world.

Now we know why astrology's never made sense,
Why all their predictions fall short of reality.
Now they can say in their own defence,
All along, there's been Sedna, unseen source of gravity.

Have you ever felt cheated at the hand you've been dealt?
Have you ever felt something's been holding you back?
It's Sedna: over six billion miles, her presence is felt,
Putting your star chart and life out of whack.

She must be the reason me and my Taurus mates
Didn't get the dream job that Cosmo Stars promised us,
Or the invites to parties, where we'd meet the hot dates,
Or all the goodies that somehow just missed us.

It's frankly a relief, knowing she is around,
Bad luck's bad enough, we need feel no shame.
Her fat ass is up there, weighing us down,
So our failures aren't ours – yes, Sedna's to blame.

But what else is out there? As our telescopes
Reach out into space, how will we cope
With a shedload of planets, destroying our hopes?
The future's unknown – a real horrorscope.

Talk Show

'He's violent, he's put me in hospital twice,
He's jealous, I cannot go out looking nice.
He's an alcoholic, he drinks all our cash,
He stays out for days with his mates, who are trash.
He's a liar, a spendthrift, lazy in bed,
Unfaithful, abusive, he's messed up me head . . .
What's that? Why'm I with him? Why don't I walk?
Well it's easy for you lot to sit there and talk!
I stay 'cos I need him, I stay for the kids,
But mostly I stay 'cos I love him to bits.'

'She cut me head open with a flung dinner plate
And when I was in prison she shagged me best mate,
She told me our last kid was some other guy's;
And everything she's said today is all lies!
She's a liar, a spendthrift, lazy, plain bad,
Unfaithful, violent, she's driving me mad.
What's that? Why'm I with her? Why not just go?
Well it's alright for you, what do you know?
I stay 'cos I need her, I stay for the kids,
Can't you all see I love her to bits!'

'I've been in some trouble, I got put into care,
Took drugs after being abused in there.
Me life's like something off Panorama,
'Cos me mam and dad were addicted to drama.
They were liars, unfaithful, had terrible fights,
Us kids lay and listened through long sleepless nights.
We couldn't stay with them, we were taken away,
No-one cared anything we had to say.
We needed them then, when we were just kids,
But they managed to love us, and each other,
To bits.'